What Do You Find in a Tide Pool?

Megan Kopp

Crabtree Publishing Company

www.crabtreebooks.com

Ecosystems Close-Up

Author
Megan Kopp

Publishing plan research and development
Reagan Miller

Editors
Janine Deschenes
Crystal Sikkens

Design
Ken Wright
Tammy McGarr (cover)

Photo research
Janine Deschenes
Crystal Sikkens

Production coordinator and prepress technician
Ken Wright

Print coordinator
Katherine Berti

Illustrations
Barbara Bedell: pages 6, 20–21, 22 (orange sea star)
Bonna Rouse: page 22 (pink sea stars)

Photographs
iStockphoto: pages 18, 19
Wikimedia Commons: Jllmob: page 3; Magnus Kjaergaard:
    page 13
All other images from Shutterstock

Library and Archives Canada Cataloguing in Publication

Kopp, Megan, author
    What do you find in a tide pool? / Megan Kopp.

(Ecosystems close-up)
Includes index.
Issued in print and electronic formats.
ISBN 978-0-7787-2263-2 (bound).--ISBN 978-0-7787-2287-8 (paperback).--
ISBN 978-1-4271-1726-7 (html)

    1. Tide pool animals--Juvenile literature. 2. Tide pool ecology--
Juvenile literature. I. Title.

QH541.5.S35K677 2016   j591.769'9   C2015-907994-2
                                                  C2015-907995-0

Library of Congress Cataloging-in-Publication Data

Names: Kopp, Megan, author.
Title: What do you find in a tide pool? / Megan Kopp.
Description: New York, New York : Crabtree Publishing Company, [2016] |
Series: Ecosystems close-up | Includes index.
Identifiers: LCCN 2015047298 (print) | LCCN 2015047594 (ebook) | ISBN
9780778722632 (reinforced library binding) | ISBN 9780778722878 (pbk.)
| ISBN 9781427117267 (electronic HTML)
Subjects: LCSH: Tide pool animals--Juvenile literature. | Tide pool
ecology--Juvenile literature. | Tide pools--Juvenile literature. |
Seashore ecology--Juvenile literature.
Classification: LCC QL122.2 .K67 2016 (print) | LCC QL122.2 (ebook) |
DDC 578.769/9--dc23
LC record available at http://lccn.loc.gov/2015047298

Crabtree Publishing Company

www.crabtreebooks.com   1-800-387-7650

Printed in Canada/032016/EF20160210

Published in Canada
Crabtree Publishing
616 Welland Ave.
St. Catharines, Ontario
L2M 5V6

Published in the United States
Crabtree Publishing
PMB 59051
350 Fifth Avenue, 59th Floor
New York, New York 10118

Published in the United Kingdom
Crabtree Publishing
Maritime House
Basin Road North, Hove
BN41 1WR

Published in Australia
Crabtree Publishing
3 Charles Street
Coburg North
VIC 3058

Contents

What is a Tide Pool?

Tides happen when water from the ocean moves in and out on beaches and rocky shores. Water covers the shore in high tide. In low tide, the water goes back to the ocean.

Much of the shore is dry in low tide.

In high tide, water covers the shore.

Tide pools form on rocky shores, like this one on Vancouver Island, Canada. They are filled with salt water from the ocean.

Pools of water

During high tide, the water brings plants and animals in from the ocean to the shore. As the water moves back out to the ocean at low tide, many plants and animals get trapped in small holes on rocky shores that stay filled with water. These water-filled holes are called tide pools.

A Tide Pool is an Ecosystem

A tide pool is a type of **ecosystem**. An ecosystem is made up of all the living and nonliving things found in one place.

*Ecosystems, such as tide pools, can be studied more closely by using **models** such as this diagram. Use the diagram to name the living and nonliving things in the tide pool.*

Sun

seaweed

rock

sea anemone

sand

sea anemone

Sea stars and sea anemones are some of the living things found in tide pool ecosystems.

sea star

All in one Place

Plants and animals are living things. Living things grow, change, and make new living things. Plants make new plants and animals have babies. Nonliving things are not alive. They cannot grow or change. Water, rocks, and sand are some nonliving things found in tide pools.

Living in a Tide Pool

A system is made up of connected parts that work together. Each part of a system has a job to do. If any part of the system is missing, the system will not work as it should. Ecosystems, such as tide pools, are systems.

All of the living and nonliving things in a tide pool are connected.

Staying Alive!

Living things need both nonliving things and other living things to **survive**, or stay alive. Plants need water, air, and food to survive. Animals need water, air, food, and **shelter** to survive. Plants and animals live only in ecosystems where they can get everything they need.

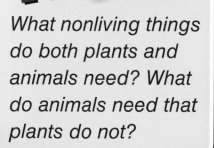

What do you Think?

What nonliving things do both plants and animals need? What do animals need that plants do not?

Crabs use rocks in tide pools for shelter.

Sea Food

All living things need food to survive. Food gives living things **energy** to grow. Plants use sunlight, air, and water to make their own food. In a shallow tide pool, sunlight easily reaches plants.

This seaweed takes in the sunlight it needs to make food.

Tasty Tide Pools!

Animals cannot make their own food. They get energy from eating other living things. Some animals eat plants. Small snails called limpets eat seaweed to get the energy they need. Some animals eat other animals. Crabs eat limpets. A **food chain** shows how energy moves from one living thing to another in an ecosystem.

crab

limpet

seaweed

This picture shows an example of a tide pool food chain. The arrows show the flow of energy.

Water In, Water Out

Tides take ocean water in and out of tide pools two times a day. Tide pool life depends on the steady in-and-out flow of ocean water.

Brown algae take in ocean water through their leaves. They need water to keep from drying out.

Tide pool fish, such as this sculpin, eat small shrimp that are carried in by the tide.

A Steady Flow

When the tide comes in, new water goes into the tide pool. This water brings in food for animals. When the tide goes out, it takes away **waste** from the tide pool.

Need Air?

Tide pool animals depend on plants to get the air they need to breathe. Tide pool plants give off oxygen into the water when they make food. Oxygen is a gas found in air and water. Animals need it to breathe.

Animals depend on plants for air. Plants depend on sunlight, air, and water to grow. This shows how living and nonliving things are connected in a tide pool.

Breathing Underwater

Most tide pool animals, such as fish and crabs, take in oxygen underwater through their gills. Gills are openings on an animal's body.

Most crabs, such as this shore crab, have gills on their legs.

What do you Think?

What would happen to the tide pool ecosystem if its plants could not get what they needed to make their own food?

Safe Shelter

Animals in a tide pool depend on living and nonliving things for shelter. Shelter is a place where animals can be safe. Some animals use shelter to hide from other animals that may want to eat them. Seaweed is a plant that gives a safe shelter for small animals to hide.

Sculpin hide by changing the colors of their bodies to blend in with rocks and plants in a tide pool.

Hold On!

Some tide pool animals need shelter to keep from being washed away or drying out when the tide goes out. Sea stars and barnacles stick themselves to rocks. Crabs hide in rocky holes. Sea anemones fold in their tentacles. Snails draw back into their hard shells.

Mussels close their shells tight to keep in water when the tide goes out.

Protecting the Tide Pool

Tide pools can be fun to explore, but they must be protected. Litter, or garbage, in or around a tide pool can hurt the plants and animals that live there.

There are many interesting things to look at in a tide pool, but be careful not to touch anything.

What do you ThinK?

Hermit crabs use other animals' empty shells for shelter. How would picking up empty shells affect the hermit crab?

Look, But Don't Touch

Touching the plants or animals in a tide pool could harm the ecosystem. Do not lift or move any rocks. The rocks might be shelter for animals. Always watch where you are walking. Stepping on a shell could destroy a snail's home.

Make a Model

A model is a **representation** of a real thing. Models can be used to explain how different parts of a system work together. Maps, pictures, storyboards, and diagrams are kinds of models.

Review how living and nonliving things in a tide pool ecosystem are connected. Then make your own model!

Ecosystems
Close Up

What Do You Find in a Backyard?
What Do You Find in a Coral Reef?
What Do You Find in a Pond?
What Do You Find in a Rainforest Tree?
What Do You Find on a Saguaro Cactus?
What Do You Find in a Tide Pool?

What Do You Find in a
Tide Pool?

Create a Tide Pool

Draw a diagram of a tide pool ecosystem to show how living things meet their needs. Remember that living things need shelter, air, food, and water to survive. Label the living and nonliving things in your diagram.

Materials you will need:
- paper
- colored pencils
- information in this book

Sunlight

Air

Seaweed

Snails

Rocks

Sea star

Crab

Include in your diagram:
- 3 living things
- 3 nonliving things

Sand

Think About It

Scientists use models to help them learn more about the systems they study. A model of a tide pool can show how each living thing gets what it needs from the ecosystem. Now it is your turn!

Choose one of the living things on your diagram. What would happen if it disappeared from the ecosystem? How would it affect other living things? Share what you have learned with your family and friends!

Sea stars in a tide pool ecosystem

Learning more

Books

Fredericks, Anthony D. *In One Tidal Pool: Crabs, Snails and Salty Tails.* Dawn Publications, 2002.

Halfmann, Janet. *Star of the Sea: A Day in the Life of a Starfish.* Henry Holt & Co., 2011.

Kawa, Katie. *Tide Pool Food Chains.* Powerkids Press, 2015.

Spilsbury, Louise. *Tide Pool: Look Inside.* Heinemann, 2013.

Websites

Monterey Bay National Marine Sanctuary: Tide Pool Life

http://montereybay.noaa.gov/visitor/TidePool/species.html

California Tide Pools

http://californiatidepools.com

Exploring the Rocky Coast of Southern Oregon Coast

www.oregontidepooling.com/tidepooling_on_the_southe/ nudibranchs/

Slater Museum of Natural History: Tidepool Sculpin

www.pugetsound.edu/academics/academic-resources/slater- museum/exhibits/marine-panel/tidepool-sculpin/

Words to know

ecosystem (EE-koh-sis-tuhm) noun all the living things in a place and their relation to the environment

energy (EN-ur-jee) noun the ability to do things

food chain (food cheyn) noun the order of living things in an ecosystem by which food energy is passed from one to another

model (MOD-l) noun a representation of a real object

representation (rep-ri-zen-TEY-shuh n) noun a picture, drawing, model, or other copy of something

shelter (SHEL-ter) noun the place where living things are safe

survive (ser-VAHYV) verb to stay alive

tide (tide) noun the constant change in sea level

waste (weyst) noun material that is no longer used

A noun is a person, place, or thing. A verb is an action word that tells you what someone or something does.

Index